SCHIRMER'S LIBRARY OF MUSICAL CLASSICS

Vol. 443

GIOVANNI BATTISTA VIOTTI

Concerto No. XXII

In A minor

For Violin and Piano

With Accompaniment of Orchestra

Revised after the Edition of

FERDINAND DAVID

by

HENRY SCHRADIECK

With a Biographical Sketch of the Author by

RICHARD ALDRICH

ISBN 978-0-7935-4949-8

G. SCHIRMER, Inc.

DISTRIBUTED BY

HAL•LEONARD®
CORPORATION
7777 W. BLUEMOUND RD. P.O. BOX 13819 MILWAUKEE, WI 53213

GIOVANNI BATTISTA VIOTTI, violinist and composer for the violin, one of the great masters of the instrument, did more than anybody else to effect the transition from the old classical Italian to the distinctively modern school. Hence his place in musical history is peculiarly important and significant, apart from the brilliant career that brought him renown as the most eminent player of his time. A pupil of Pugnani, who was himself a pupil of Corelli's pupil Somis, and Tartini, Viotti came into the rich heritage of the great Italian traditions; and it seems almost like the irony of fate that he should have been the one to do the most in effecting the transfer of supremacy in the violin from the ancient domain of Italy to France and Germany. His own genius at the same time made important contributions to the great fabric of modern art, both in its technique and in the formal resources that have developed the solo concerto in its modern sense; and he is to be named by the side of Mozart as producing the first concertos of this kind that have endured to the present time.

Viotti was born in Fontanello, a little Piedmont village, on March 23, 1753, the son of a blacksmith of musical proclivities who played on the French horn. From him and from a wandering musician named Giovannini the boy—precociously clever in his display of talent, like most who have become great musicians—learned the elements of music; and by the time he was eight years old was taking delight in playing upon a little fiddle procured for him from the local fair. When he was thirteen his talent was brought to the notice of the Bishop of the diocese, who sent him to Turin to study, and had him placed in charge of Pugnani, with whom he made rapid progress. His master esteemed his powers highly, for in 1780 he took him on a tour through Northern Europe. They visited Germany, Poland and Russia, later England and France; and everywhere young Viotti's playing aroused great enthusiasm. In Paris he parted company with his master, to continue his brilliant career alone. He first appeared there in one of the Concerts Spirituels in 1782, and created a profound impression. His playing seemed almost like the revelation of a new art. "Never," says Fétis, "had playing been heard that approached this perfection; never had any artist exhibited a finer tone, an elegance so unfailing, such brilliancy and variety." Here he appeared with triumphant success for two years. The passing caprice of the public, that on one occasion seemed to prefer to him a violinist of inferior rank, so disgusted him that he thereupon resolved never to appear again in public. He remained in Paris, however, enjoying the special favor of the Queen and of the great world of fashion and art, composing and participating in the private concerts of the noble patrons of music as player and conductor.

In 1788, after an unsuccessful attempt to secure the management of the Opéra, he joined Léonard, the Queen's hairdresser, who had obtained a license to establish an Italian opera, undertaking the musical direction. A brilliant company was gathered, and the enterprise started with success; but the outbreak of the Revolution soon brought it to disaster. Viotti lost everything he had, and betook himself to London, where he began again his career of a virtuoso, appearing at the Hanover Square concerts under the noted Salomon, in several new concertos that he had written especially for them. Falling under quite undeserved suspicion of being an agent in England of the French revolutionists, he found himself compelled to leave the country, and took refuge near Hamburg, where he lived for some time in retirement. He returned to London, however, in a few years, and, in 1794, entered the troubled waters of Italian opera, which have brought to shipwreck so many managers in London. In addition he conducted and played frequently in concerts; when Haydn made his famous visit to London in 1794 and 1795, Viotti was leader of the orchestra at his benefit-concerts. But the opera involved him in financial difficulties; and these, with his growing aversion to public playing, finally led him to abandon his career altogether, and to embark in the wine-trade. He continued to compose, however, and to this period of his life belongs the last and best series of his concertos. He made two visits to Paris: one in 1812, when he yielded to the persuasion of his friends and played in public some of these later concertos; and again in 1818, when he made a longer stay, and was appointed director of the Opéra, then sunk deep in decadence. He tried for three years to raise it to a higher level, but unsuccessfully; and in 1822 resigned and returned to London, where he died in 1824.

Viotti's concertos were his most important compositions. He wrote twenty-nine, several of which still live in the repertory of modern violinists; the twenty-second is the most famous, appealing to modern taste more than the rest through its fine subjects and the symphonic treatment of the orchestral accompaniment. It gives, perhaps, the most characteristic exemplification of the advances he made in the writing of concertos. These advances, in which he went hand in hand with Mozart, consisted in extending the form to the broader dimensions which it now has, developing it after the model of the sonata, and elaborating the accompaniment with the full resources of the orchestra of his time. He wrote also two concertantes for two violins, twenty-one string-quartets, twenty-one string-trios, fifty-one violin-duets (still highly esteemed and much used in instruction), eighteen sonatas for violin and bass, and one for violin and pianoforte. As a player, Viotti had an influence on his contemporaries second only to that of Corelli and Tartini before him and Spohr after him. He had a few pupils of distinction, chief among whom were Rode and Baillot, who transmitted his influence to the later and greater generation of artists.

RICHARD ALDRICH.

Concerto № 22.

Edited by
Ferdinund David.

Revised by
Henry Schradieck.

G.B.VIOTTI.

Moderato.

Piano

⊕ vi=de ⊕ means that passages between these signs may be omitted.

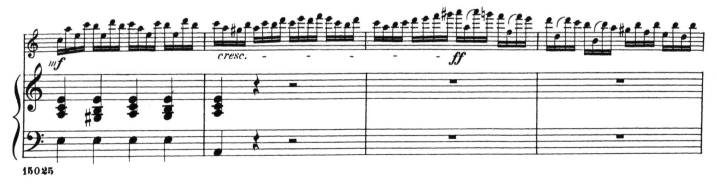

Concerto № 22.

Explanation of the Signs.

⊓ = Down-bow.
V = Up-bow.
I = E-string.
II - A-string.
III = D-string.

IV = G-string.
nut = at the nut.
pt. = at the point.
fb. = full bow.
hb. = half bow.

mb.= in the middle of the bow.
sh. = short stroke.
br. = broad stroke.

Edited by
Ferdinand David.

Revised by
Henry Schradieck.

Violin.

G. B. VIOTTI.

⊕ vi = de ⊕ means, that passages between these signs may be omitted.

15025

Violin.

Violin.

Violin.

Violin.

Violin.

Violin.

Violin.

9

15025

10

Agitato assai.

Violin.

15025

Violin.

Violin.

Violin.

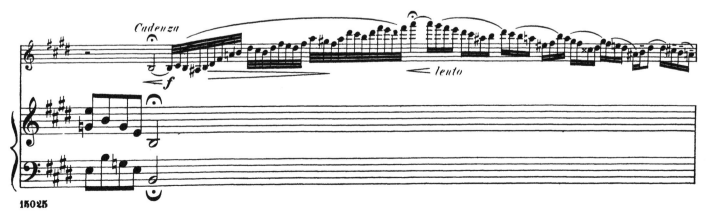

15025

15025

15025

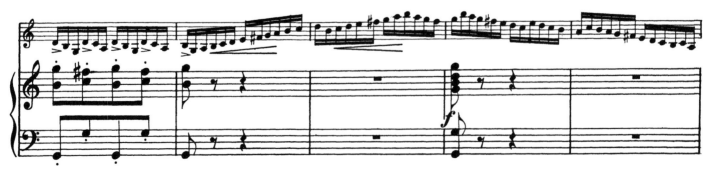

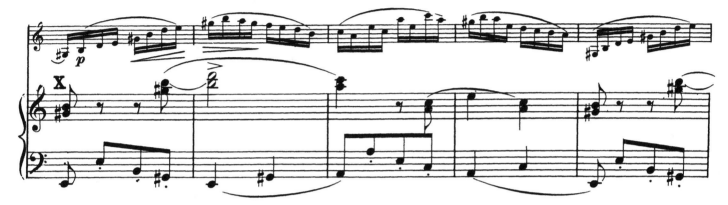

15025